you're in the right place
at the right time
with the right book

visual
WORD
ART
puzzles

letters of
one word
drawn together
harmoniously

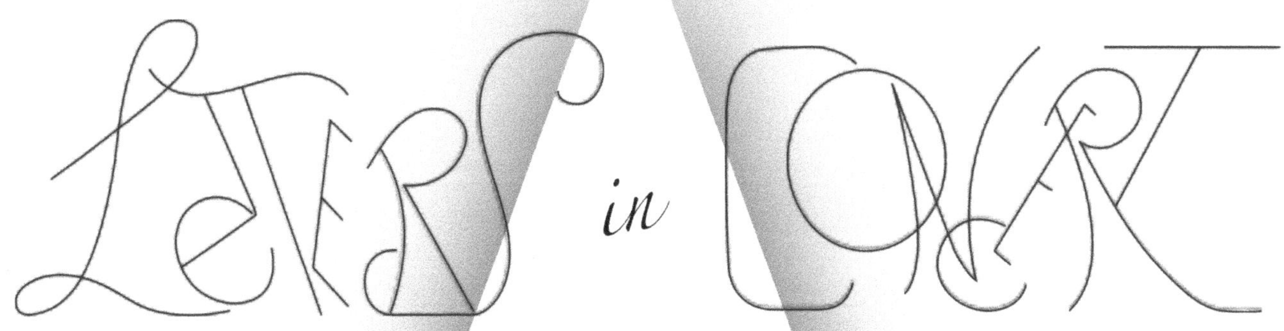

welcomes
you

with

LOVE

to its resonant

CREATIVE

ENERGY

find the letters

1ˢᵗ
activity

8 - 29

tracing & coloring

2ⁿᵈ
activity

30 - 51

freestyle

3ʳᵈ
activity

52 - 58

ACTIVITY 1

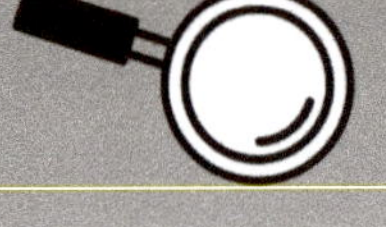

WHERE ARE THE LETTERS 
WHAT IS THE WORD

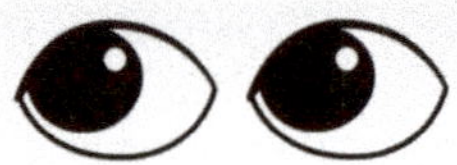

Most of the LETTERS are connected without overlapping & they're all CAPITALIZED

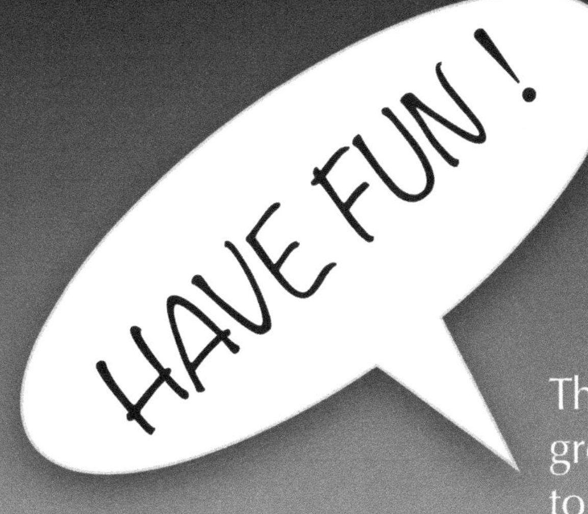

This is a challenging activity for group settings. Set up a time limit to discover the word.

This is also a fun spelling exercise for children, making learning new words more enjoyable.

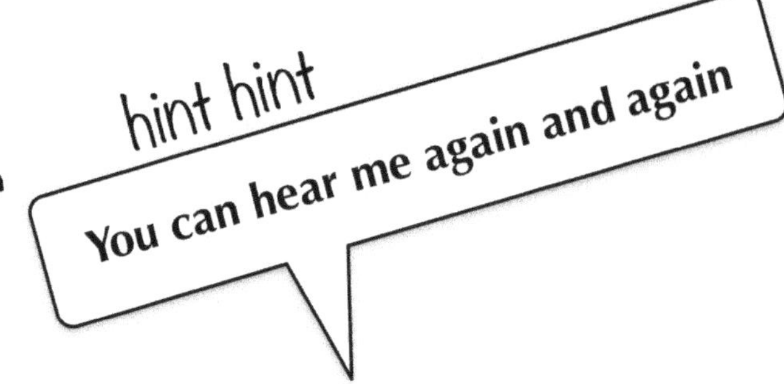

- - - - - -

4 letter word drawing

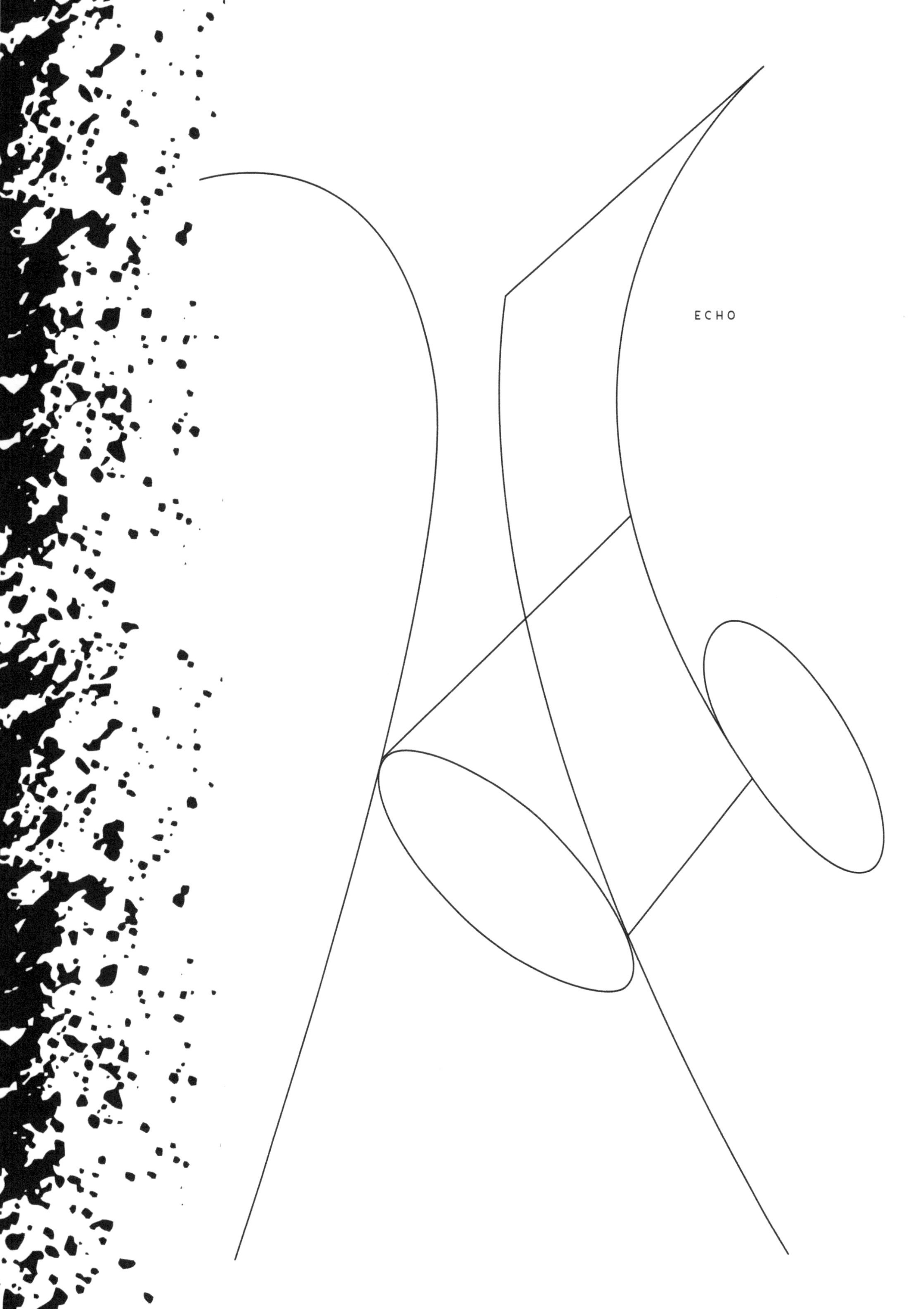

ECHO

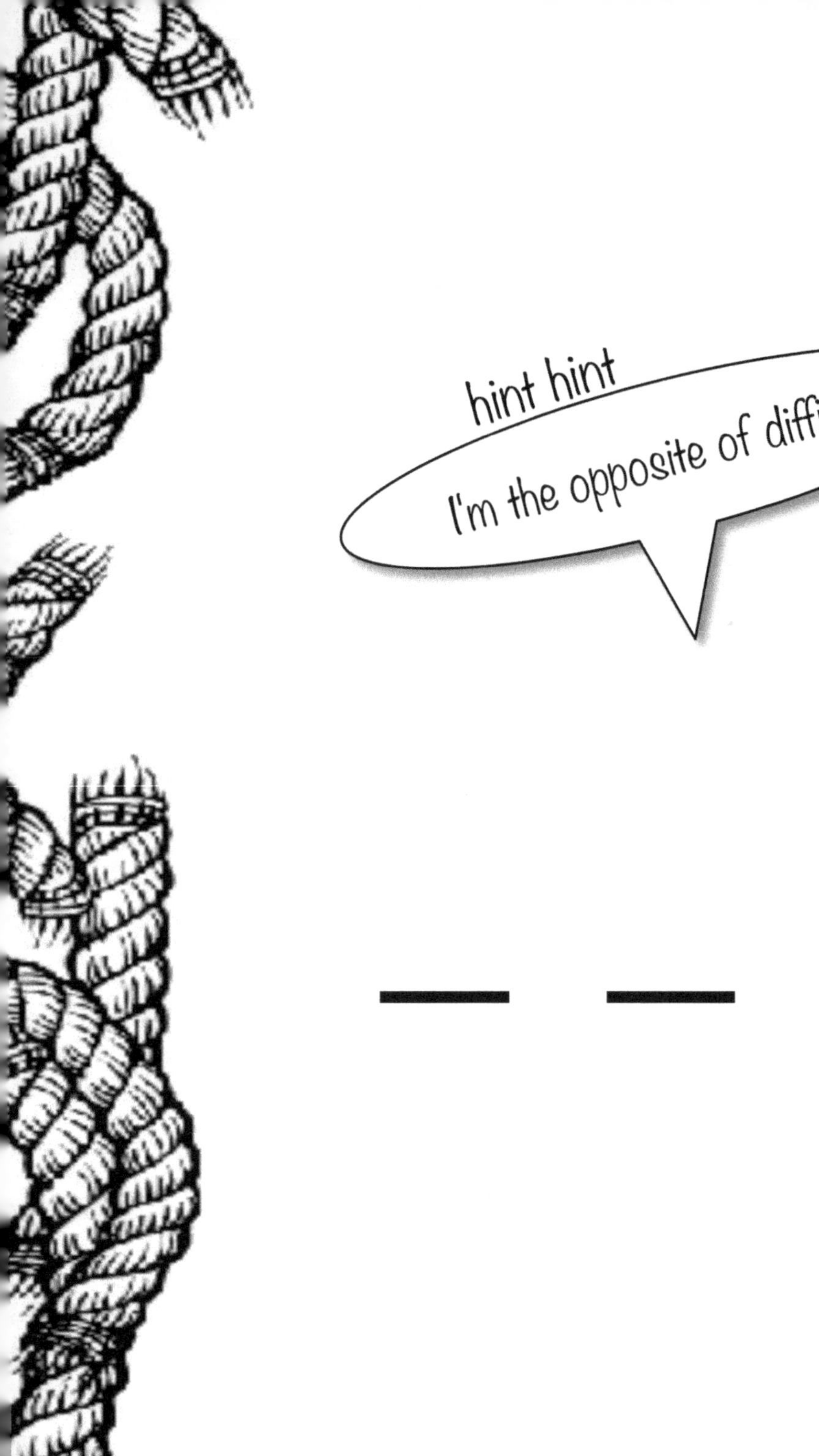

— — — —

4 letter word drawing

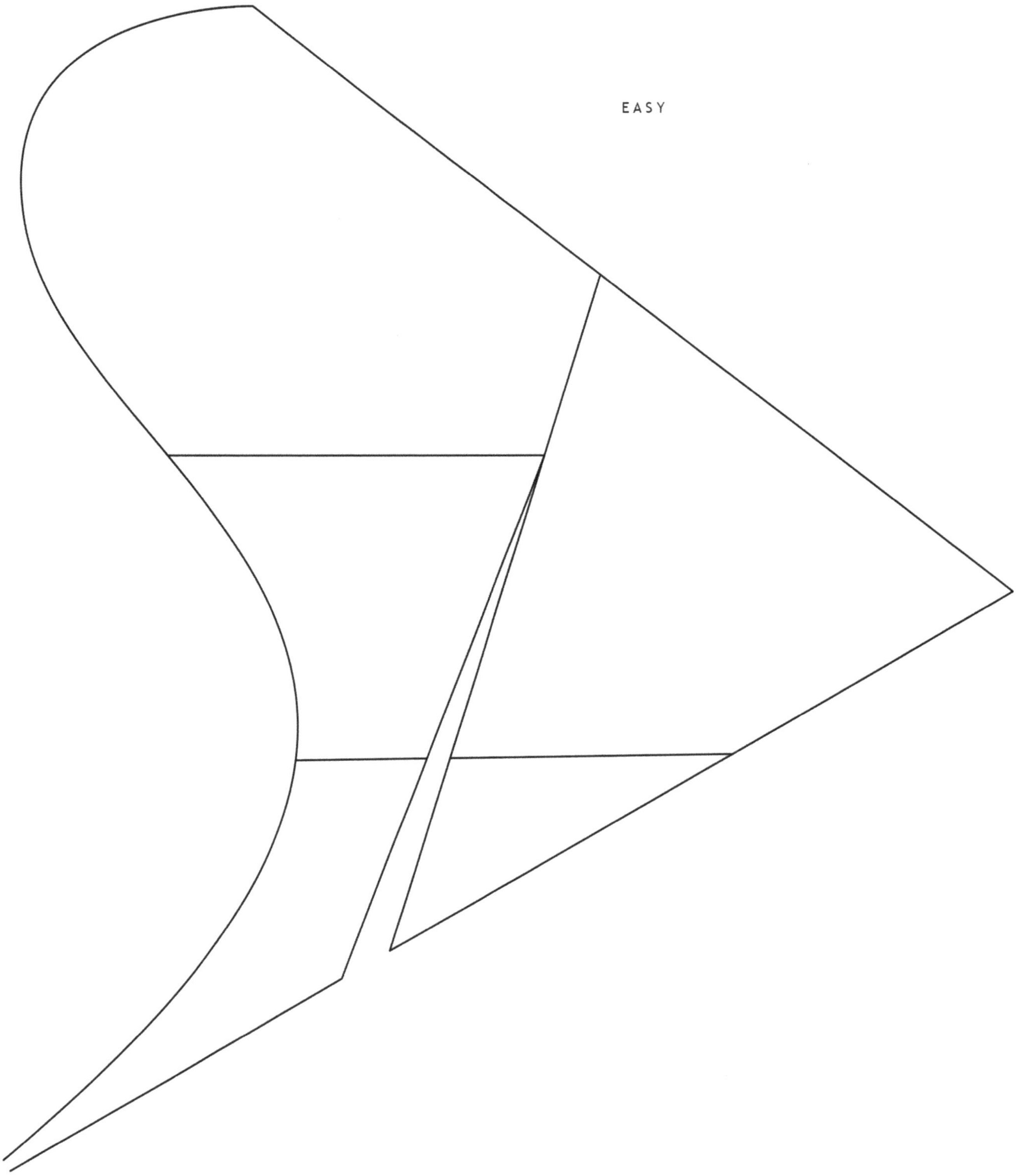

EASY

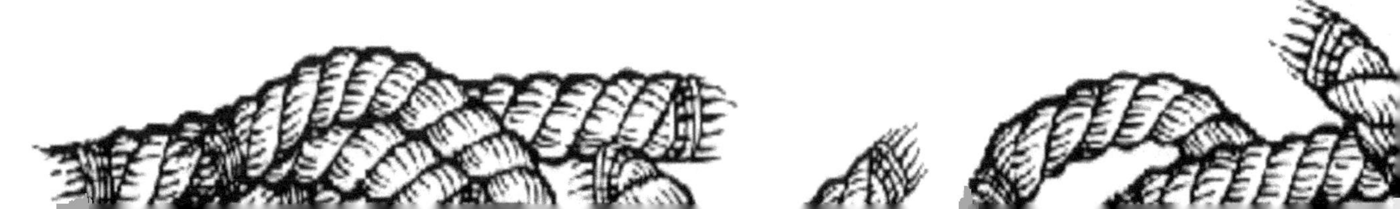

_ _ _ _

4 letter word drawing

DO YOUR BEST BEFORE SEEING THE LETTERS - LAST PAGES OF THE BOOK

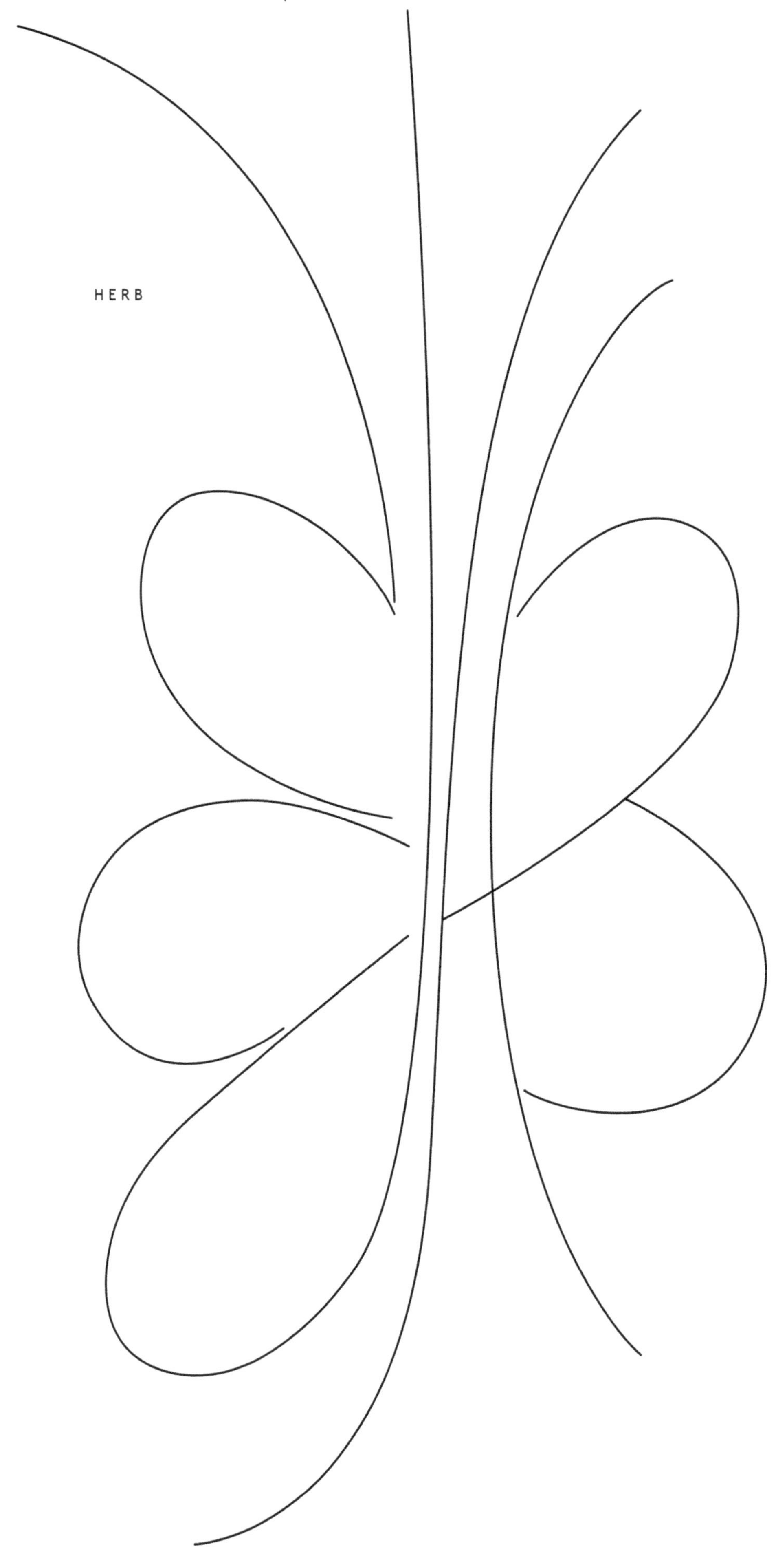

HERB

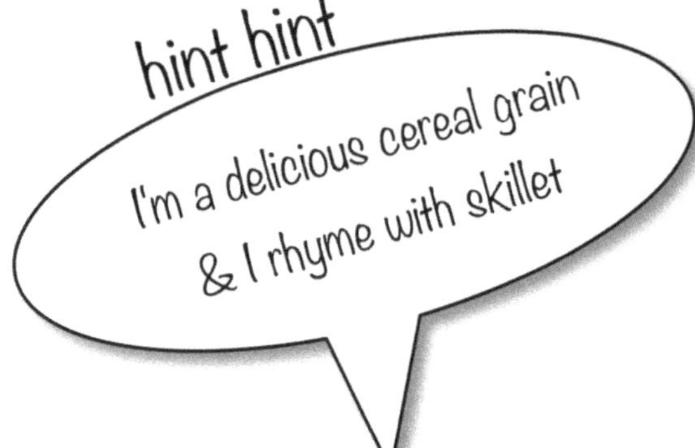

_ I L _ E _

3 letter drawing

DO YOUR BEST BEFORE SEEING THE LETTERS - LAST PAGES OF THE BOOK

page 16

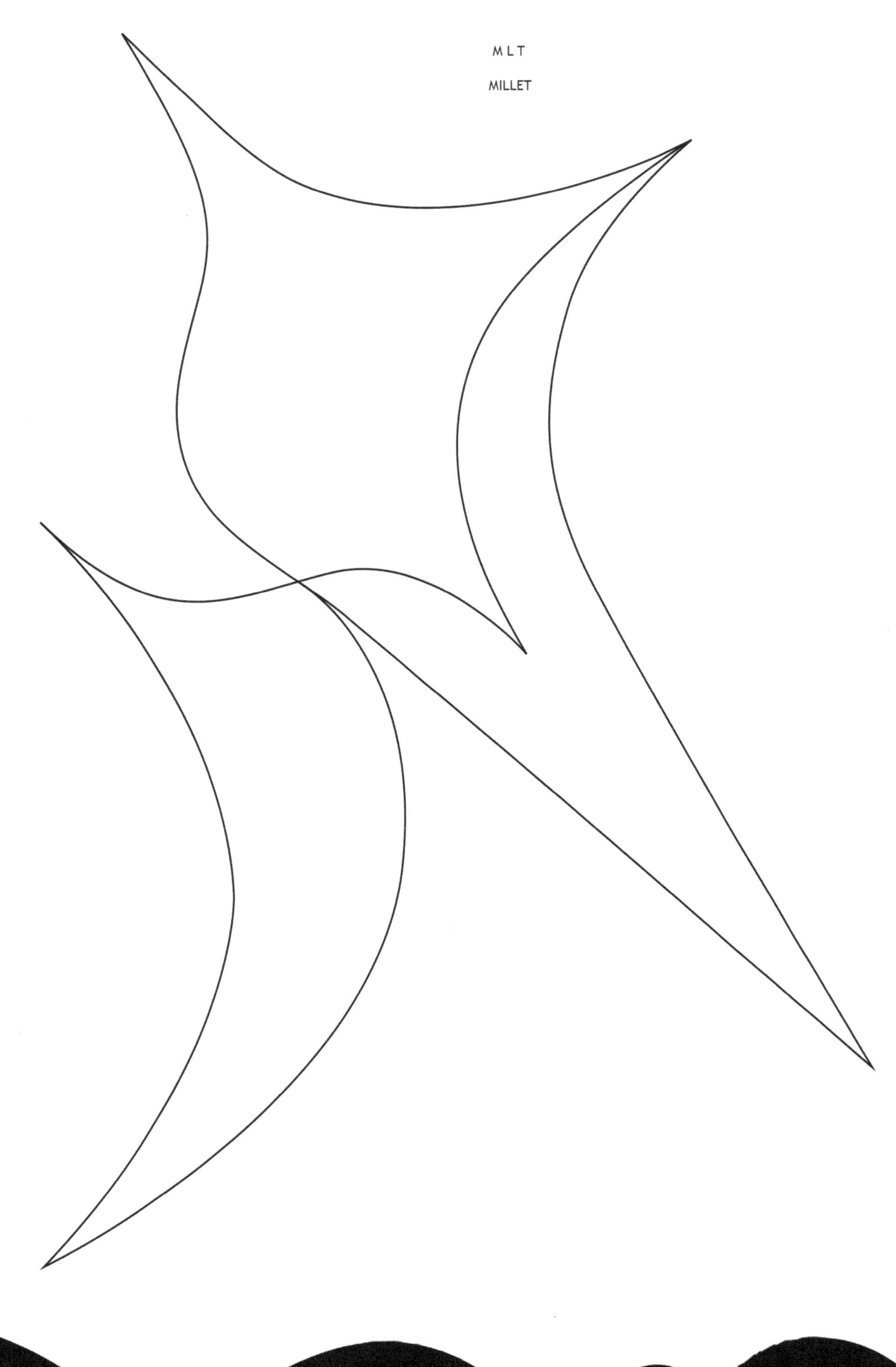
M L T
MILLET

— — — —

3 letter word drawing

DO YOUR BEST BEFORE SEEING THE LETTERS - LAST PAGES OF THE BOOK

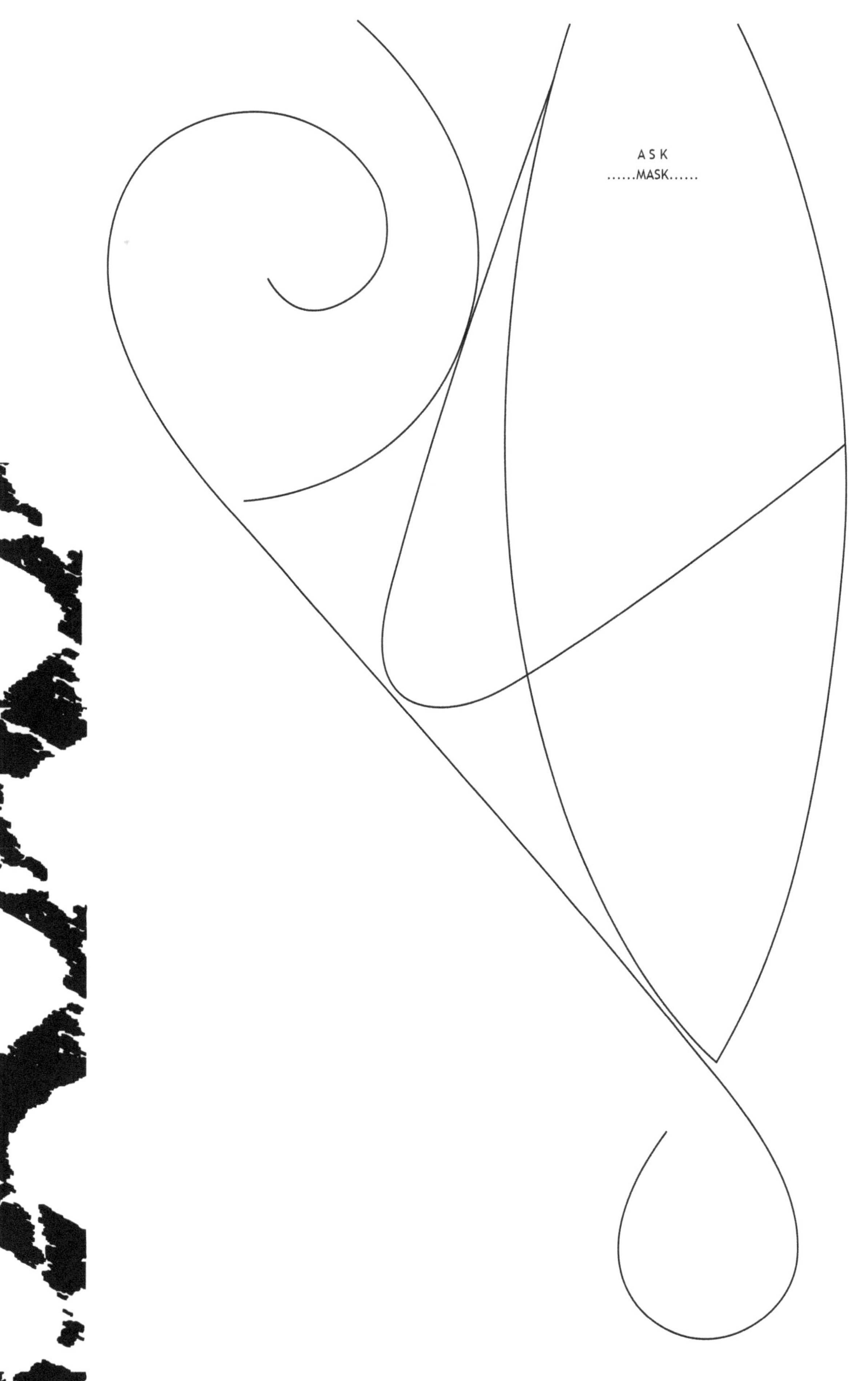
A S K
......MASK......

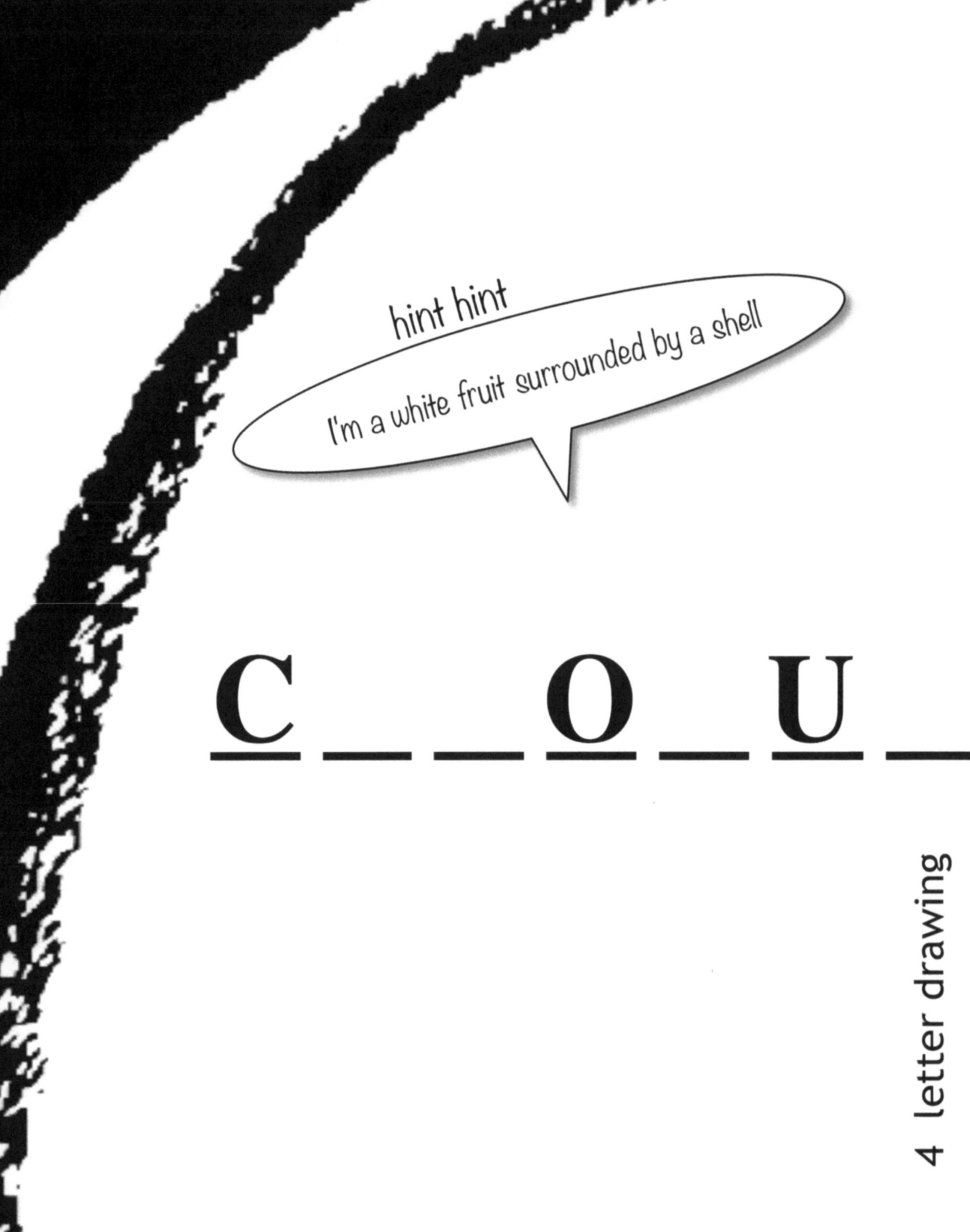

C _ _ _ O _ U _

4 letter drawing

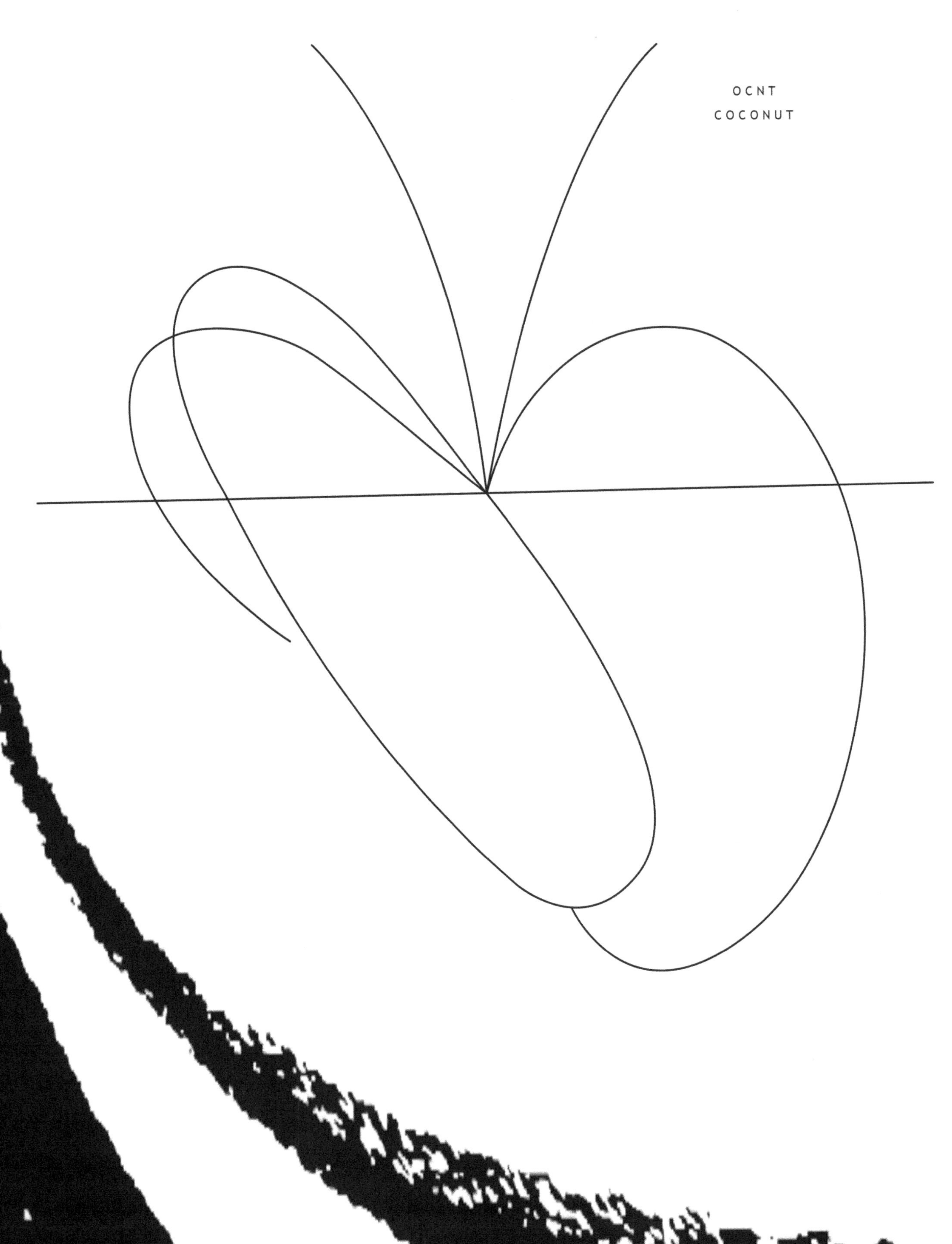

OCNT
COCONUT

5 letter word drawing

DO YOUR BEST BEFORE SEEING THE LETTERS - LAST PAGES OF THE BOOK

page 22

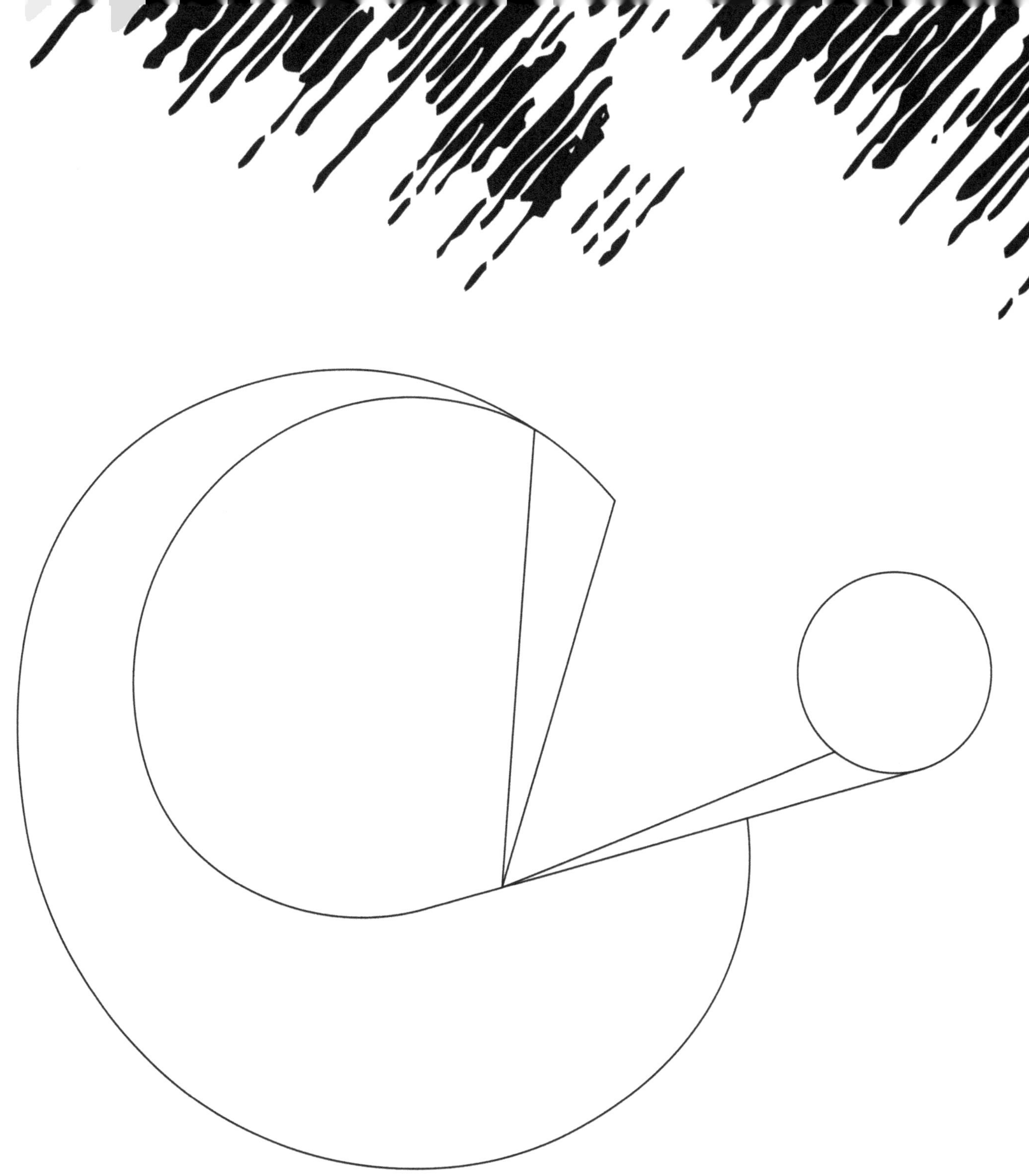

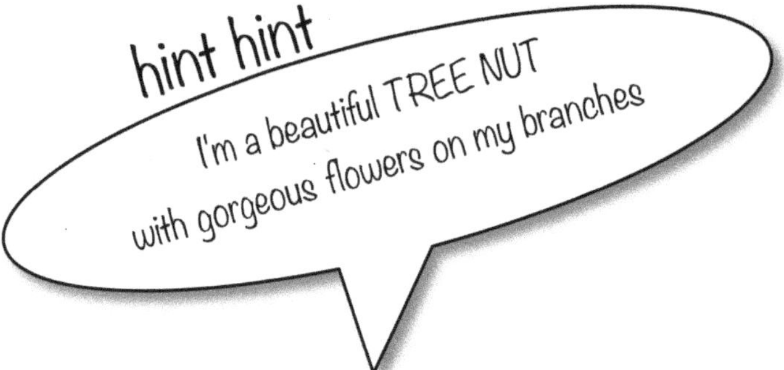

A _ _ _ O _ D

3 letter drawing

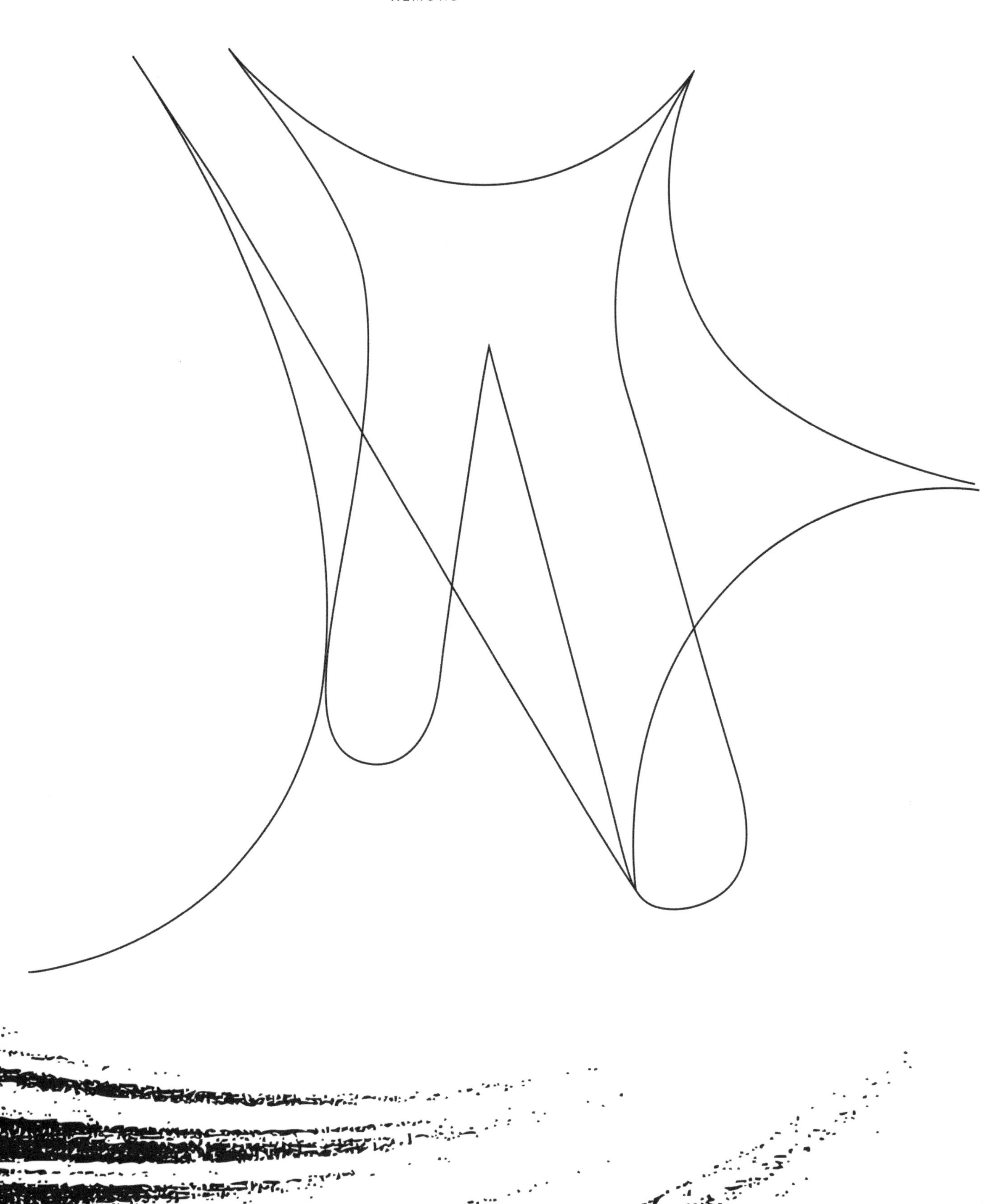

LMN
ALMOND

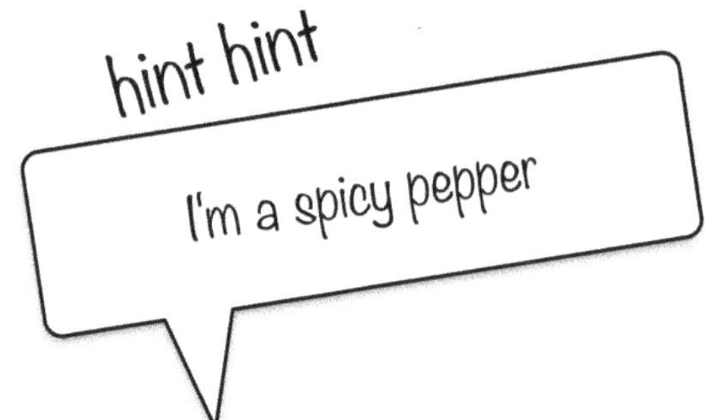

_ A _ _ E _ N _

4 letter drawing

DO YOUR BEST BEFORE SEEING THE LETTERS - LAST PAGES OF THE BOOK

page 26

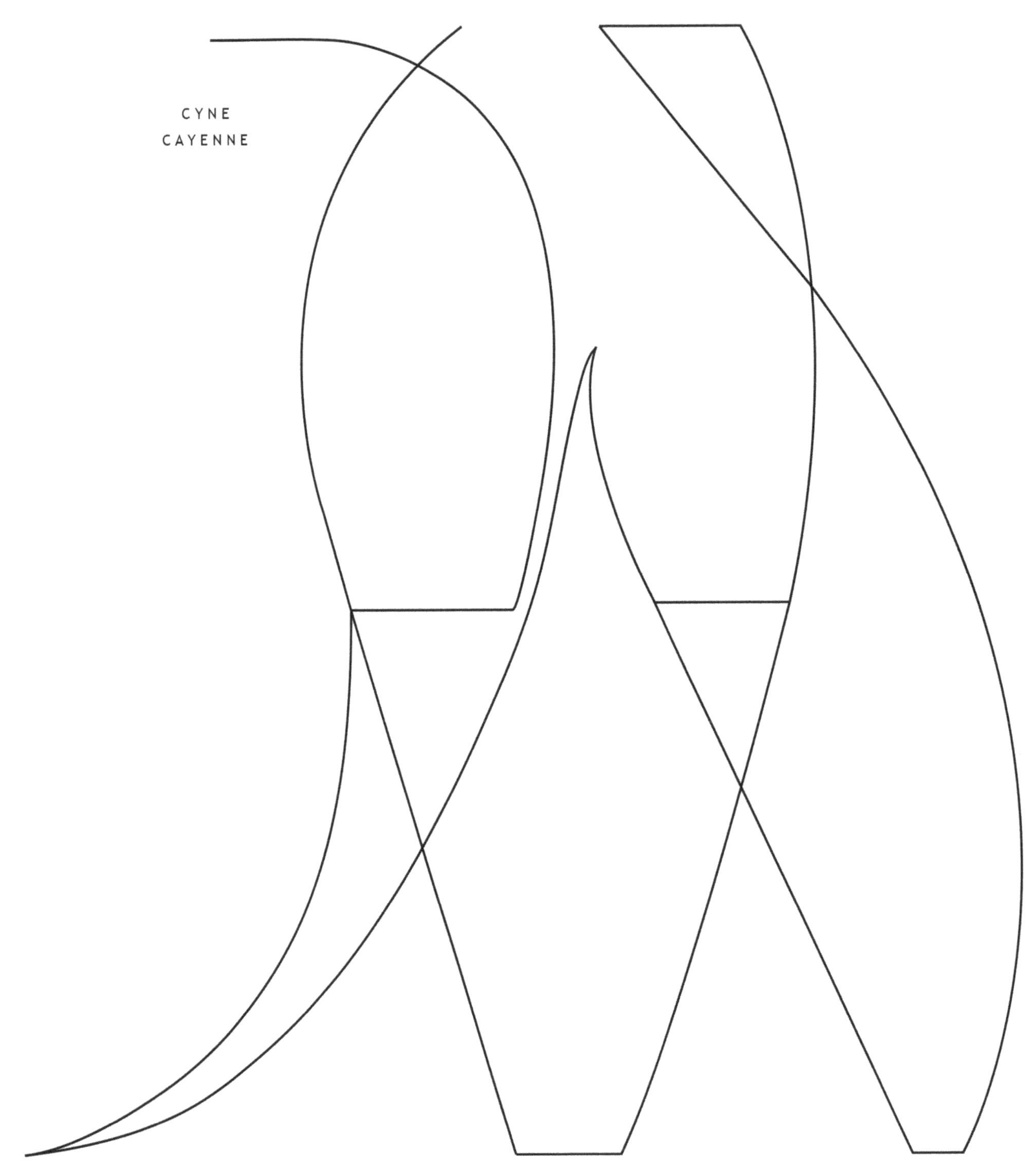
CYNE
CAYENNE

8 letter word drawing

DO YOUR BEST BEFORE SEEING THE LETTERS - LAST PAGES OF THE BOOK

page 28

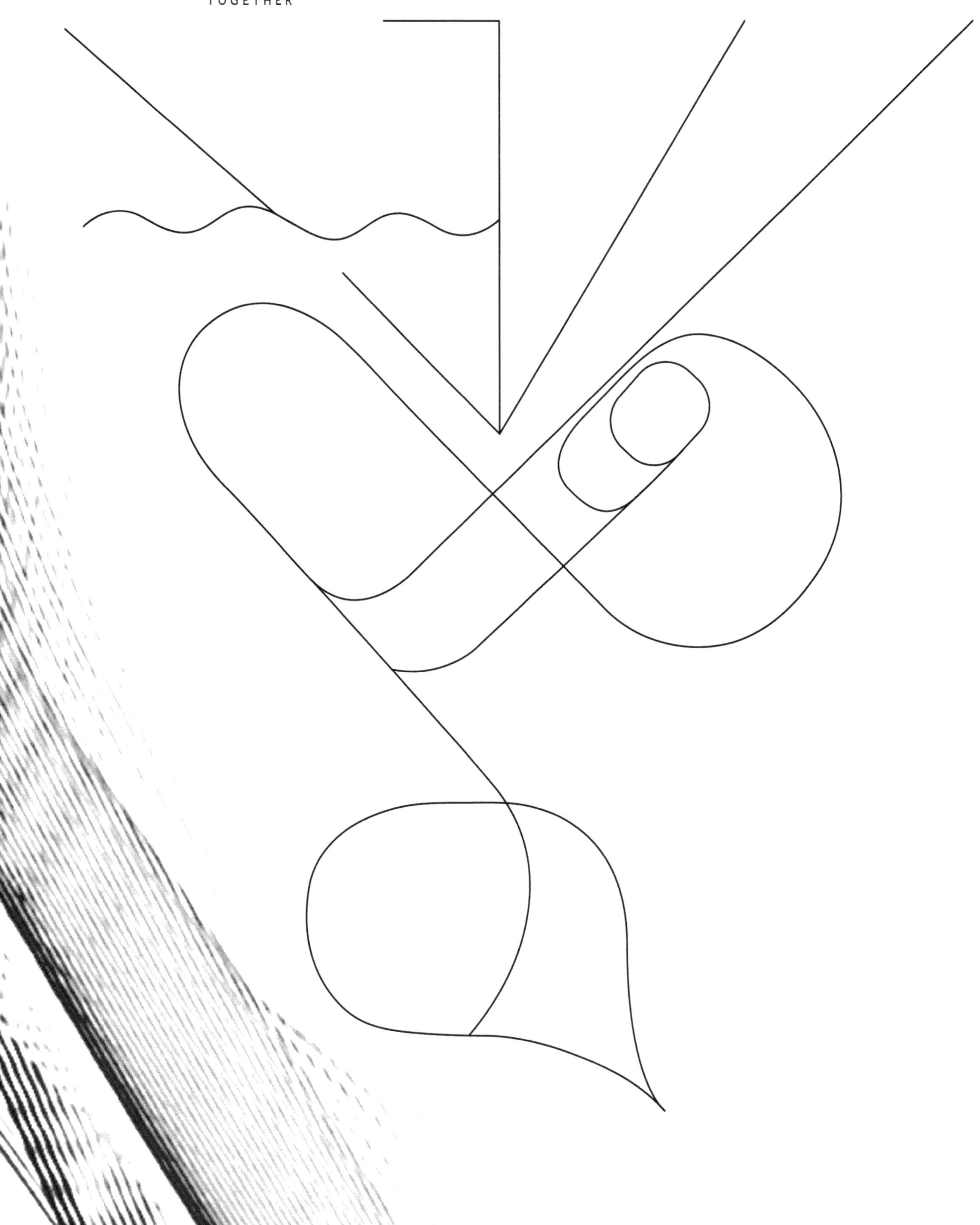
TOGETHER

ACTIVITY 2

TRACING & COLORING

ENJOY
the soothing influence of tracing & coloring

ESCAPE
into a world of relaxation

ADD
dimension with your colorful touch

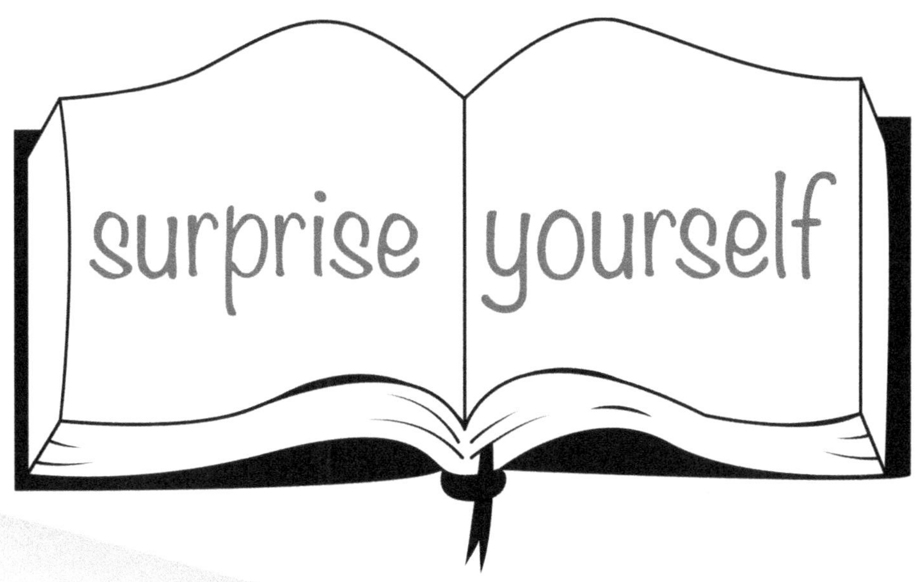

Beautiful Frame

Build a Gallery Wall set

Collage/Decoupage

Invite others to collaborate

Share the flair

Perfect gifts and delightful Coffee Table Books

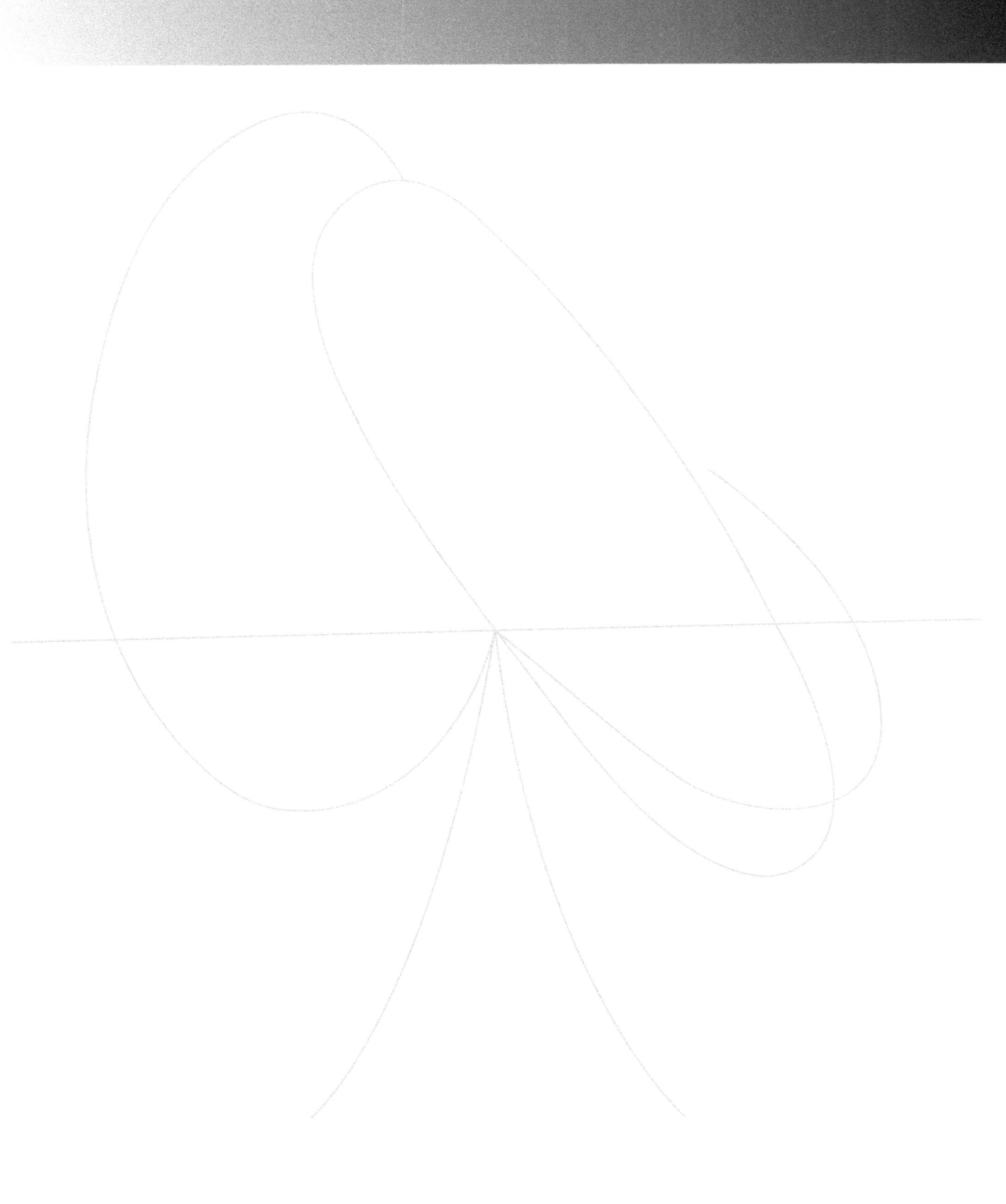

ACTIVITY 3

FREE *Letters* in *Cursive* STYLE

GET READY your pencil

SET your eraser on the side

GO slow, enjoy each moment

VIVE LE DESSIN !

a **M**agical process

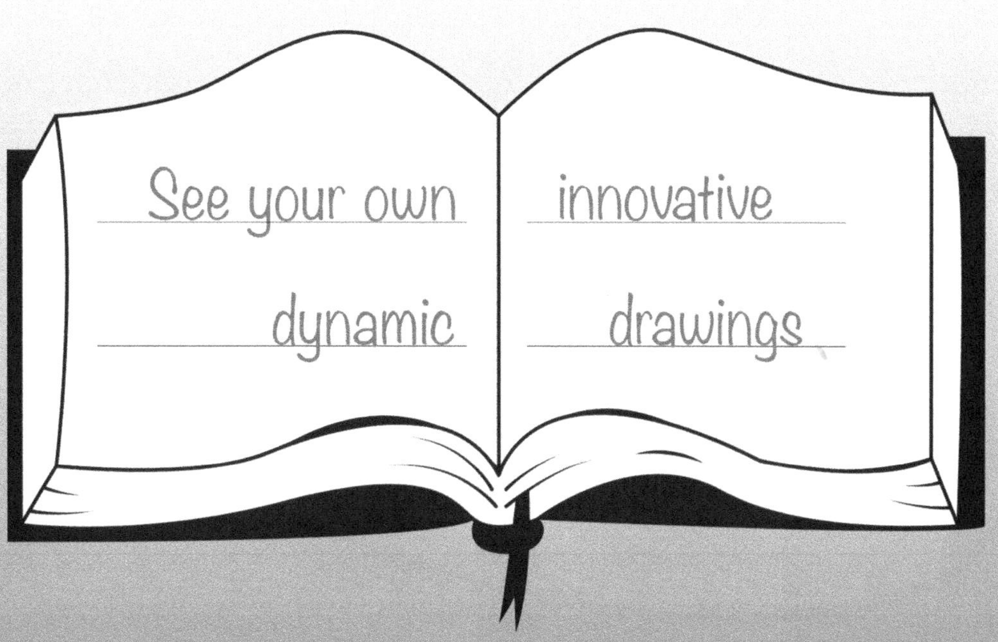

**Surround yourself by the beauty
of nature for inspiration**

**Use shapes & shadows of your favorite
artifacts as a point of reference**

Erase & shift as many times as you like

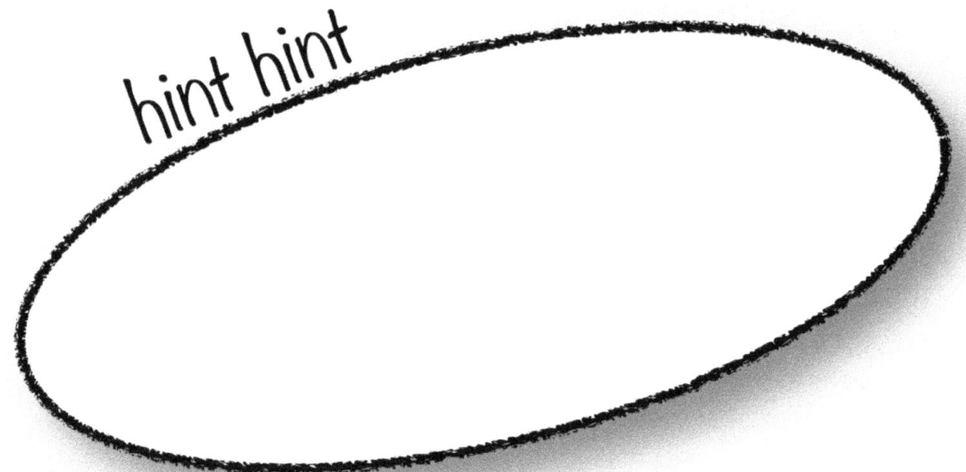
hint hint

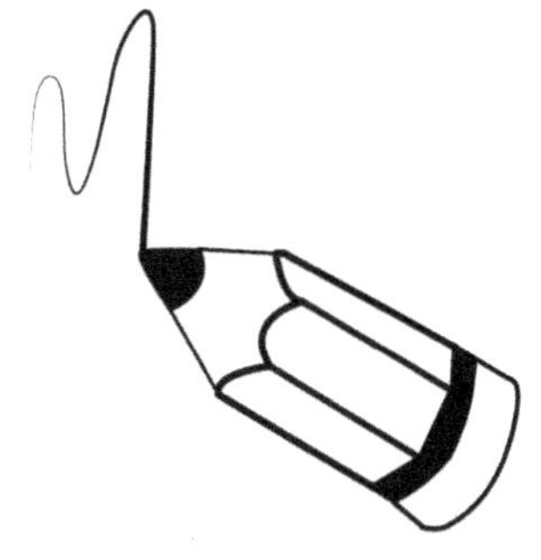

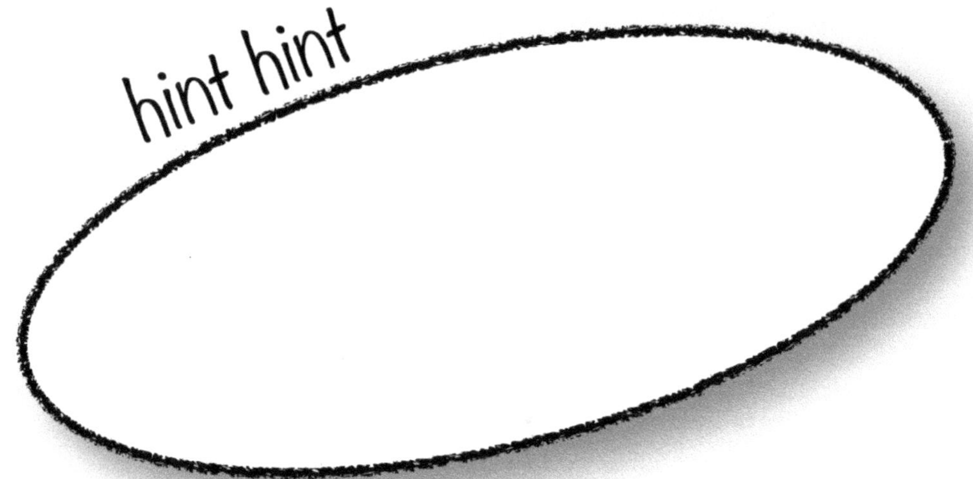

hint hint

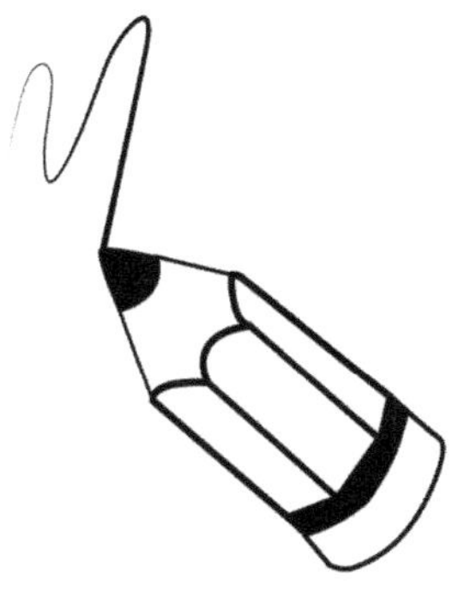

Pop-up
Pop-up
Pop-up
Pop-up

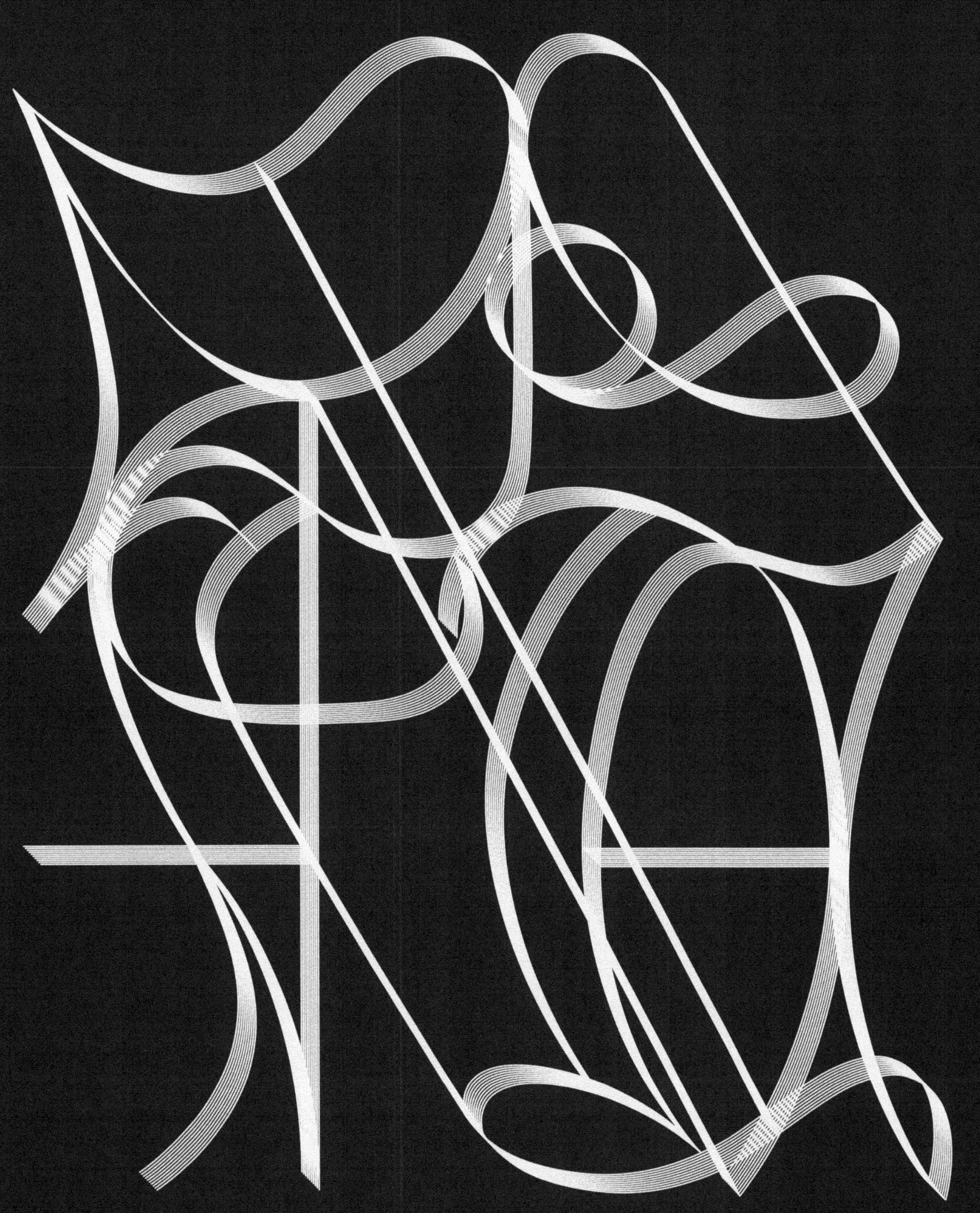

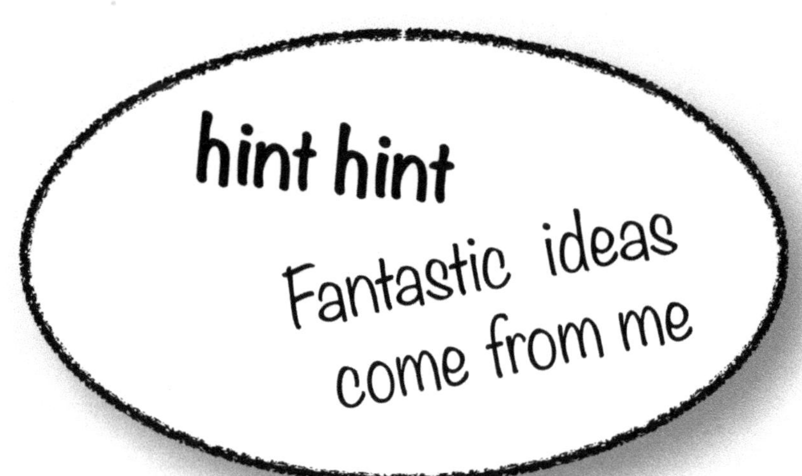

write all the letters that you see in the drawing.   Write them in any order.

Unscramble the letters you wrote above and guess what the word is.
Do your best before turning the page.

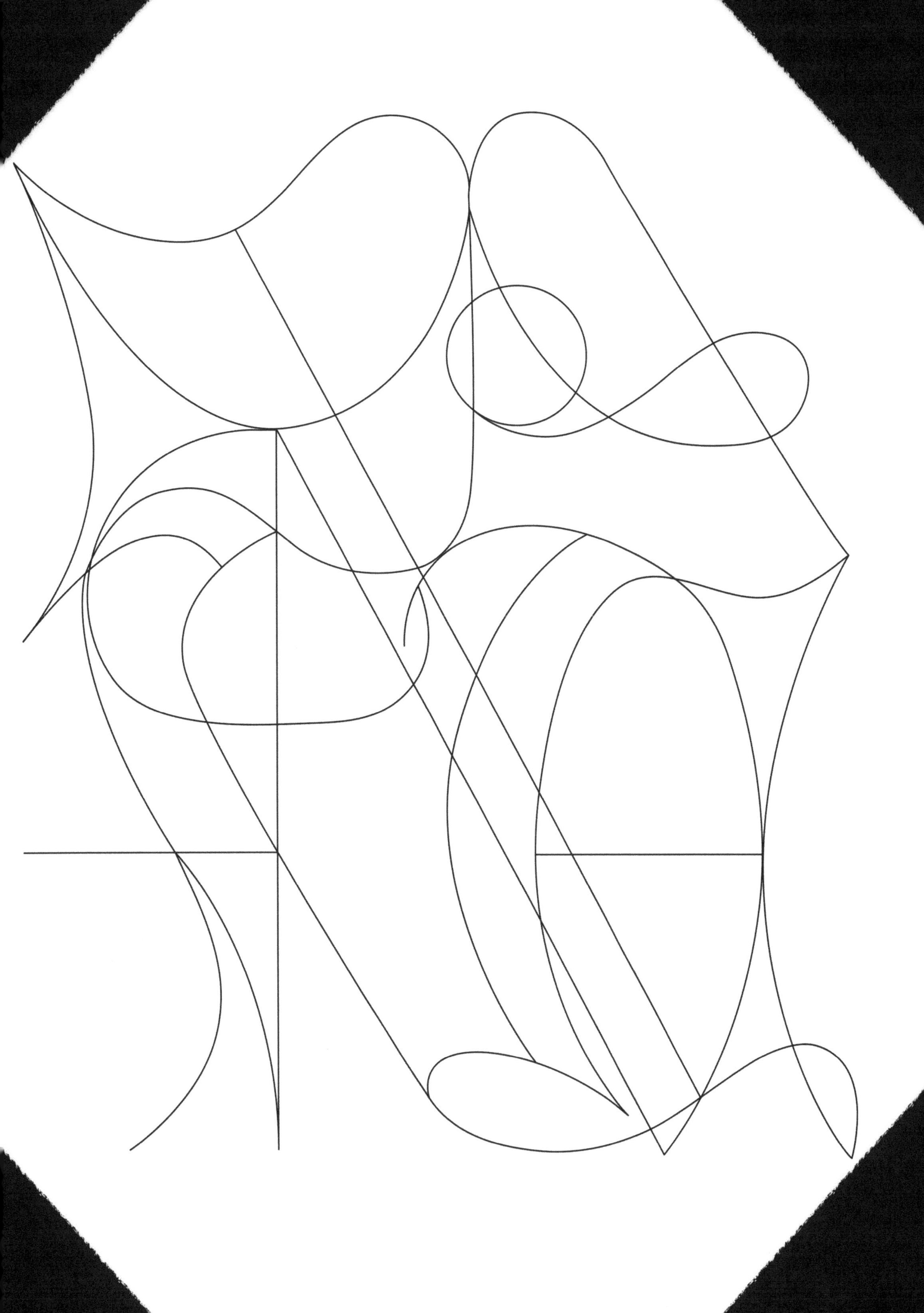

IMAGINATION

page 62

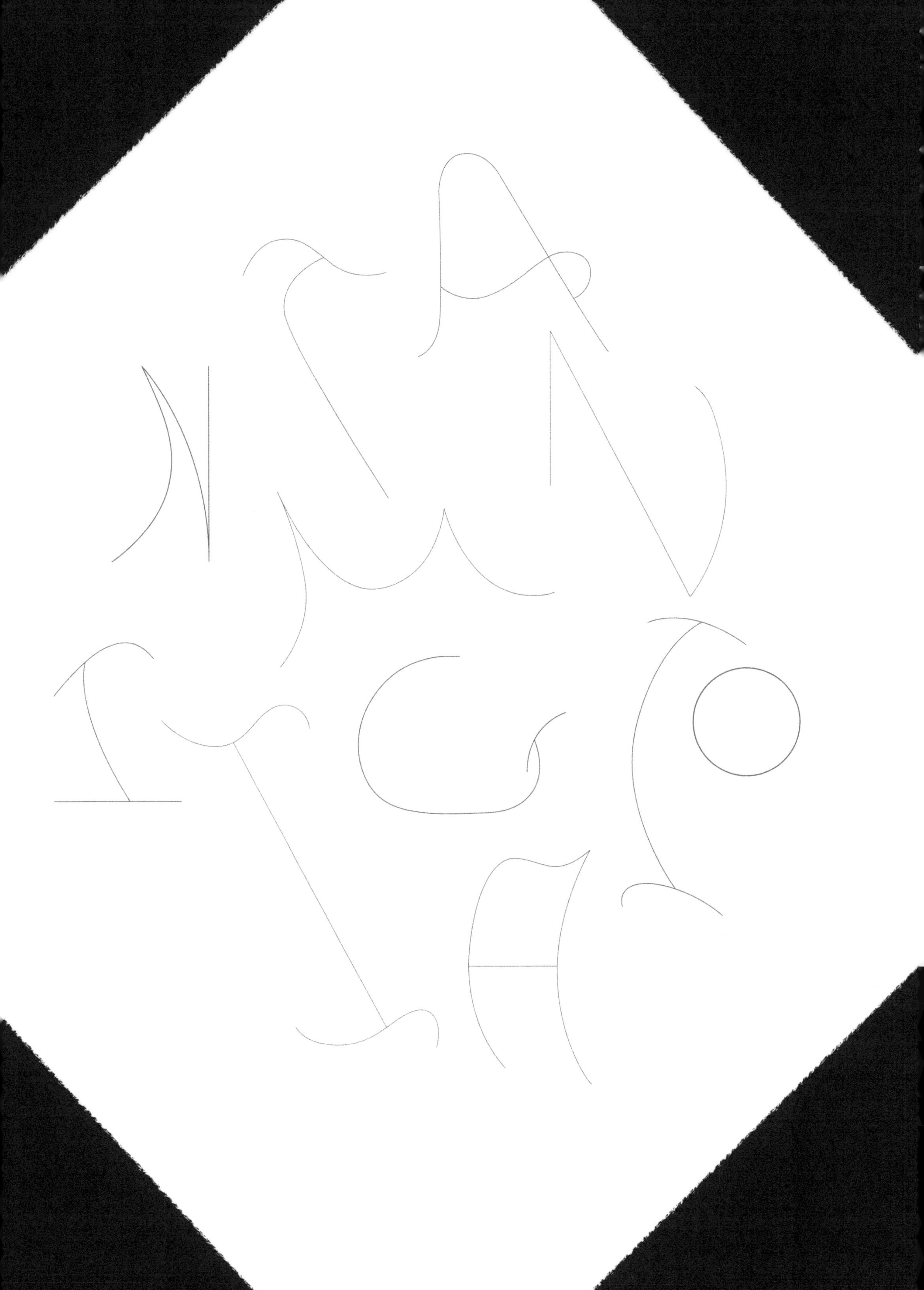

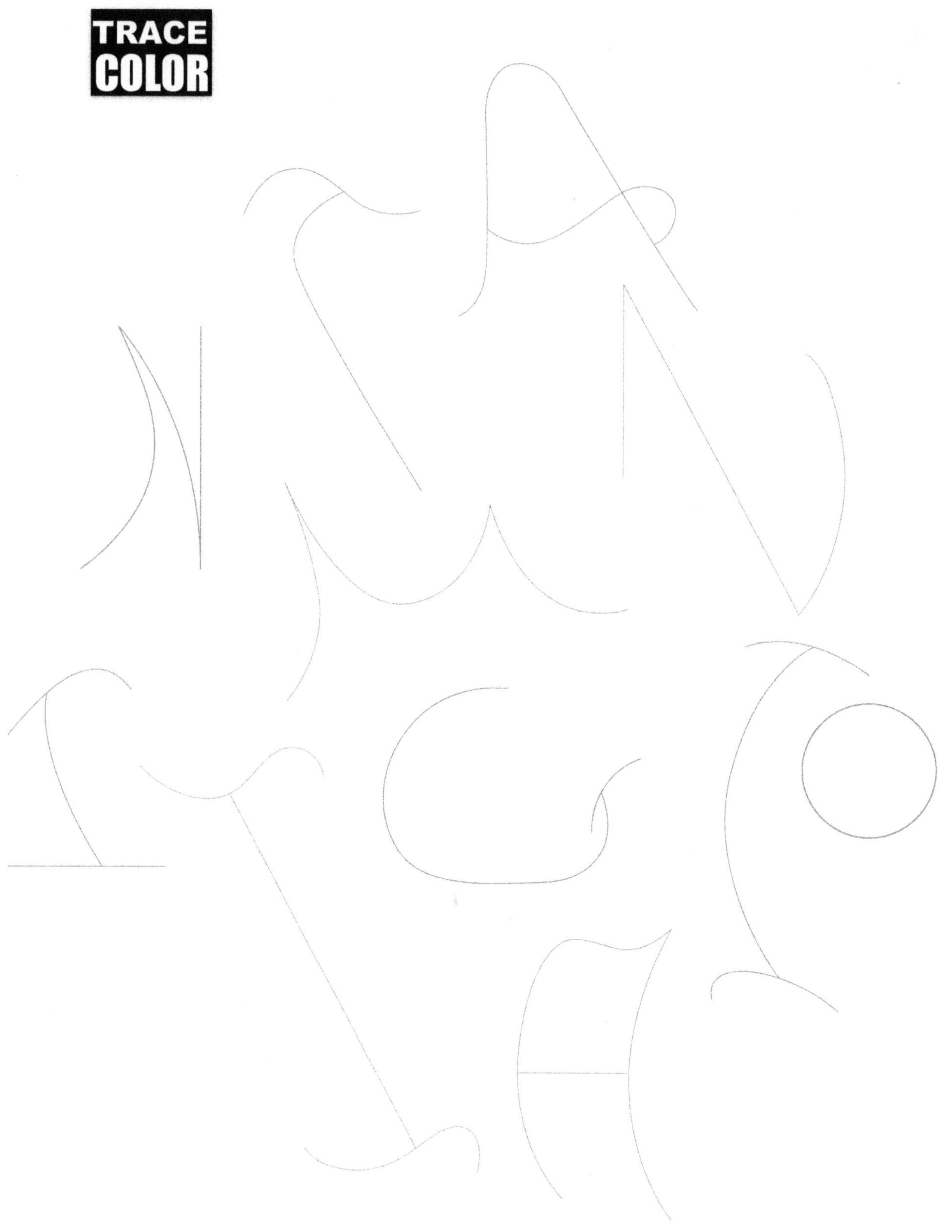

page 64

COLOR
TRACE

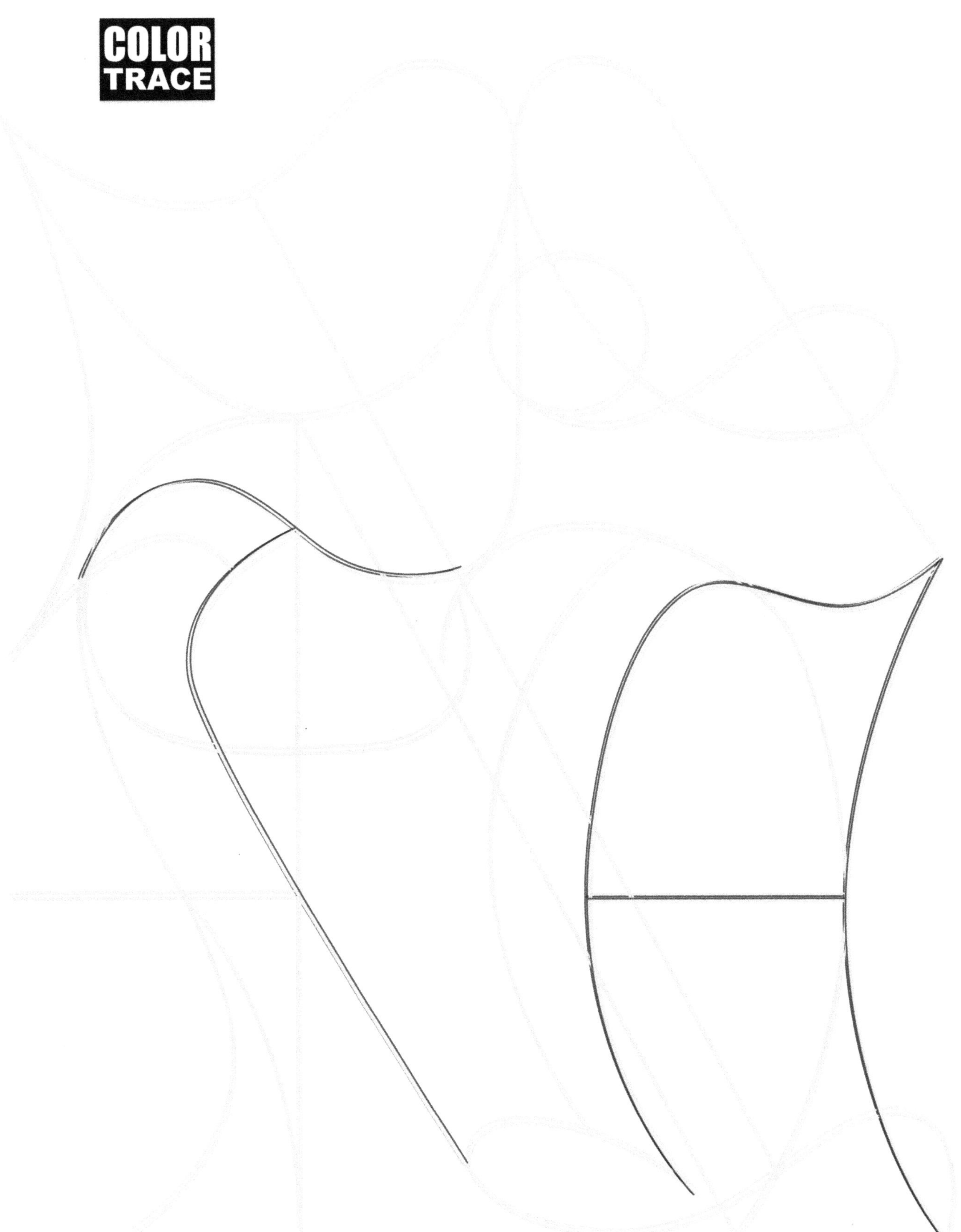

thank you
for playing
Letters In Concert

see a
myriad of
imaginative
drawings

Activities
to FILL
moments
with
FUN

Heart of Love

Gift of time

Place of beauty

The drawings in books 4 to 10 would still
be in my souvenir box if it weren't for my
daughter who inspires me constantly

I love you B & C and may the
blessings of justice & kindness
reign on all sentient beings

Thank you Siende Joshua
You're a brilliant graphic designer
& a magnificent person

Letters in Concert

aligns
lines
with

the
Beauty
of the
unexpected

YOUR GIFT →

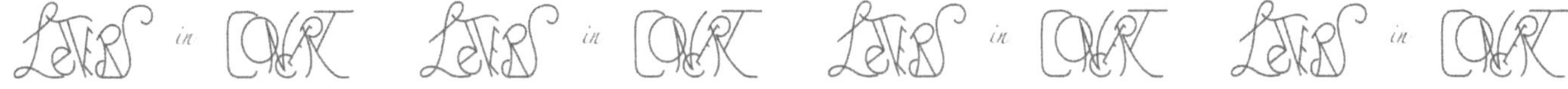

Receive a drawing in
'Letters In Concert' style
Word of your choice

Go to **www.lettersinconcert.com** to send your word

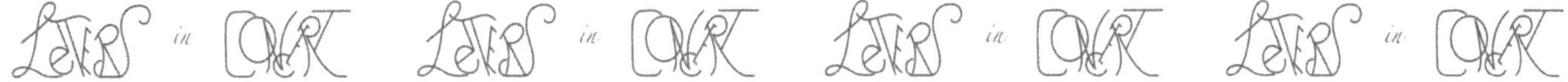

Letters in Concert   Letters in Concert   Letters in Concert   Letters in Concert   Letters in Concert

Letters in Concert   Letters in Concert   Letters in Concert   Letters in Concert   Letters in Concert

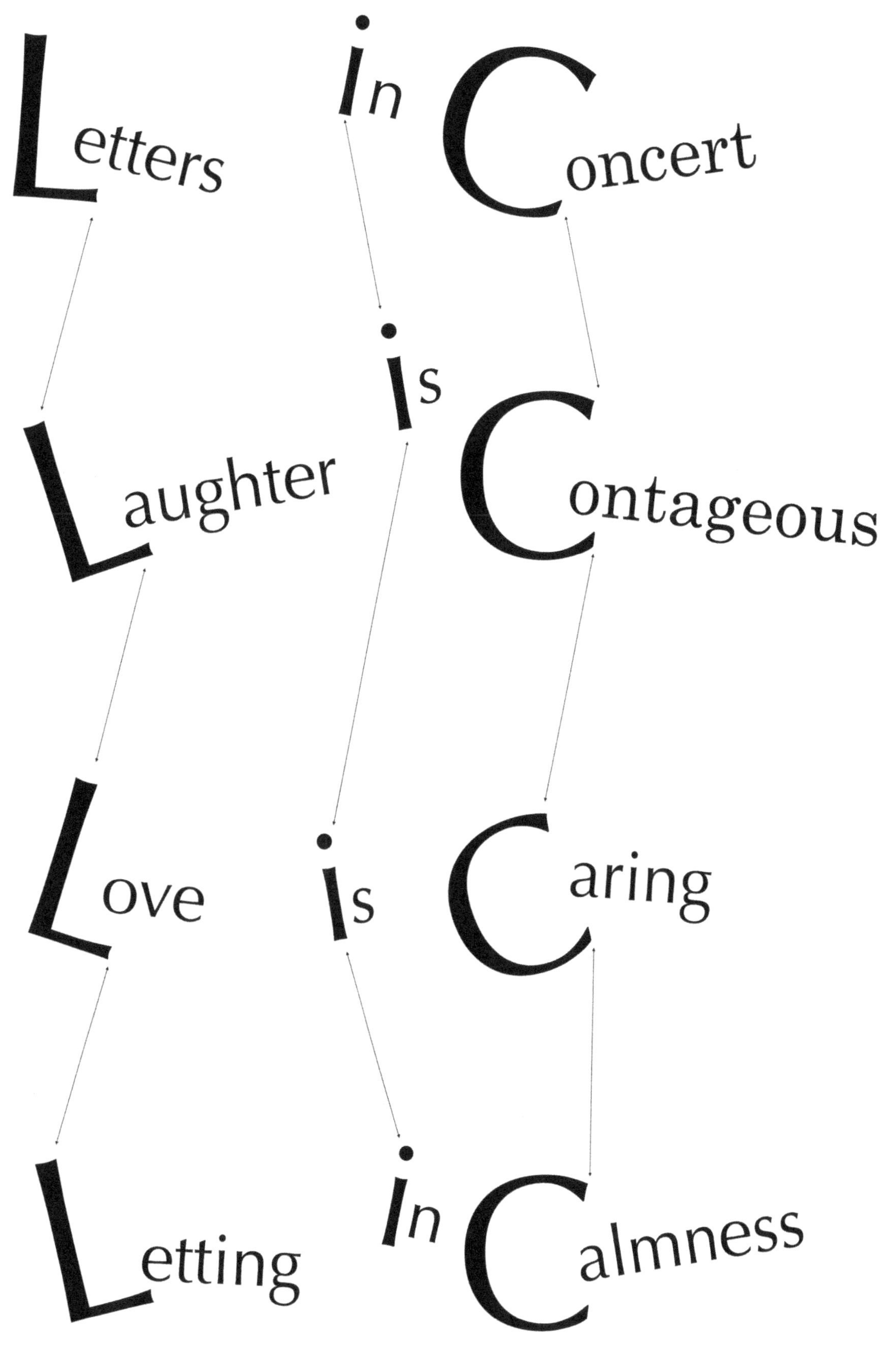

Letters
In Concert
Laughter is Contageous
Love is Caring
Letting in Calmness

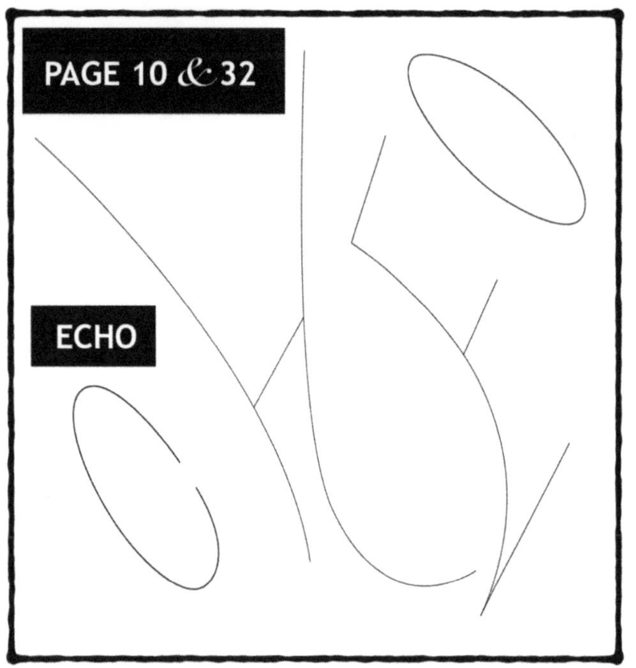

PAGE 10 & 32
ECHO

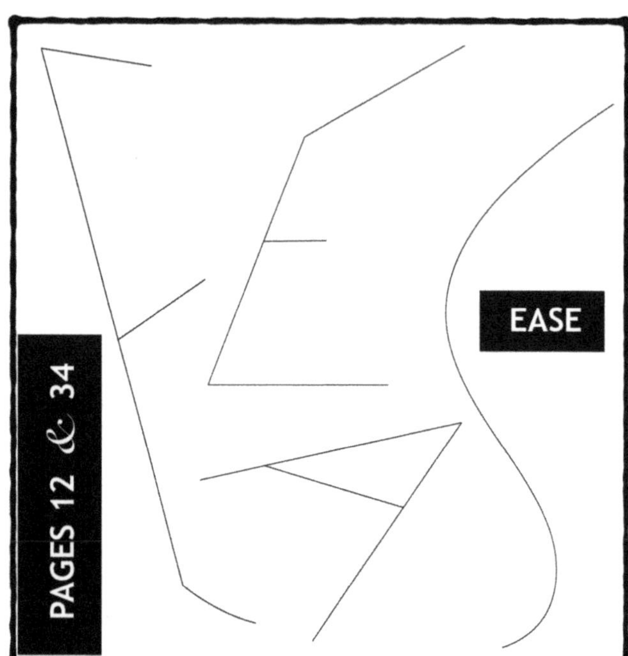

EASE
PAGES 12 & 34

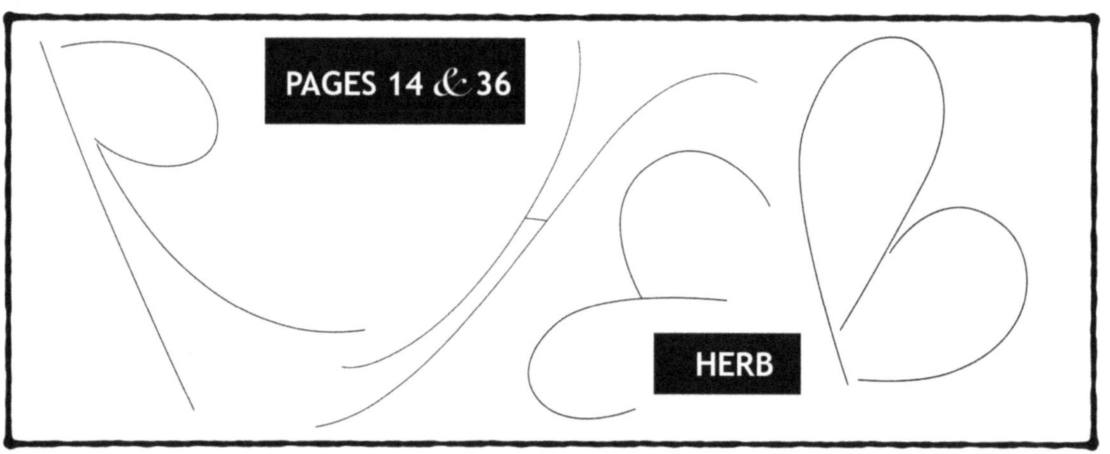

PAGES 14 & 36
HERB

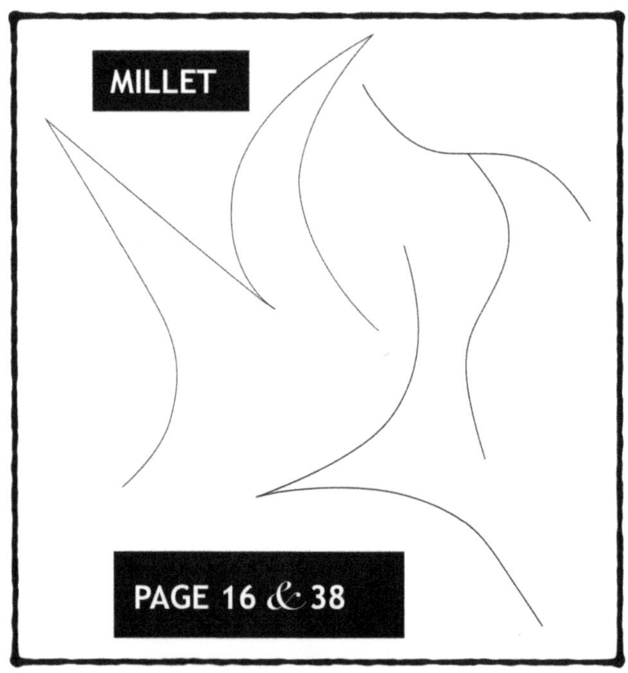

MILLET
PAGE 16 & 38

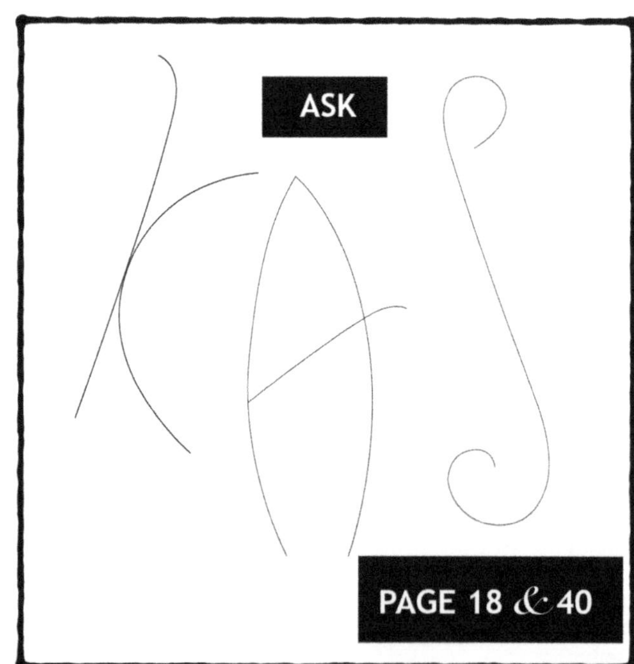

ASK
PAGE 18 & 40

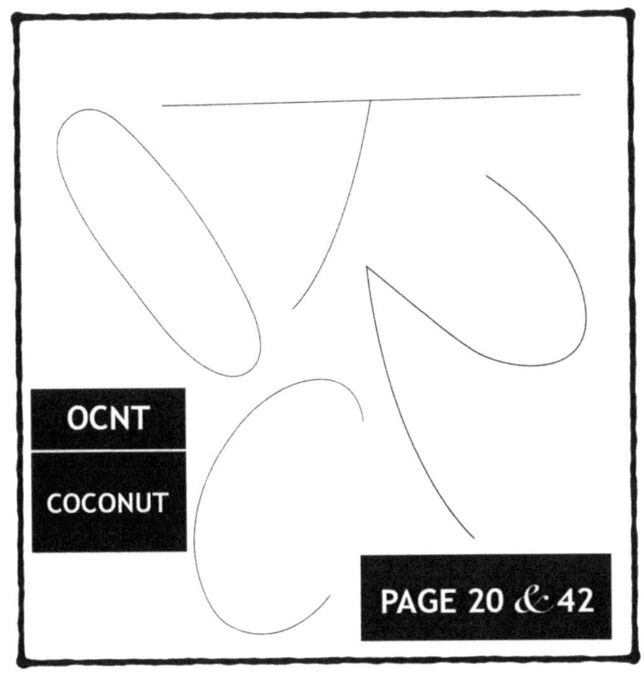

OCNT
COCONUT

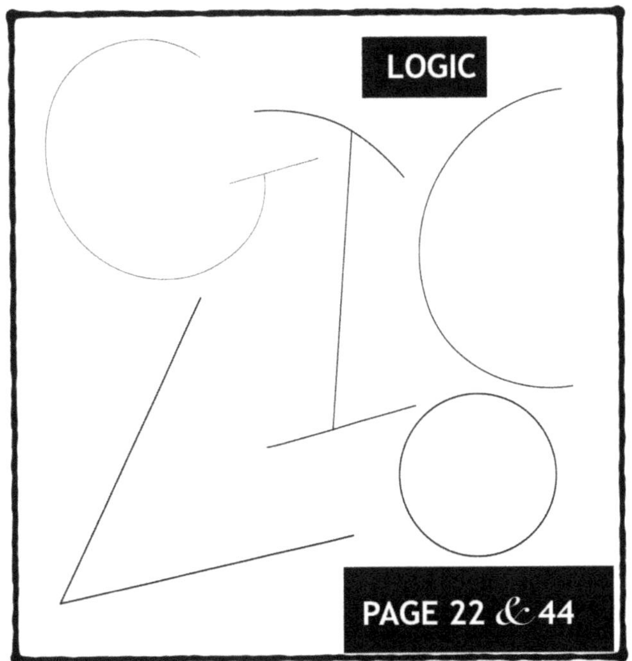

LOGIC

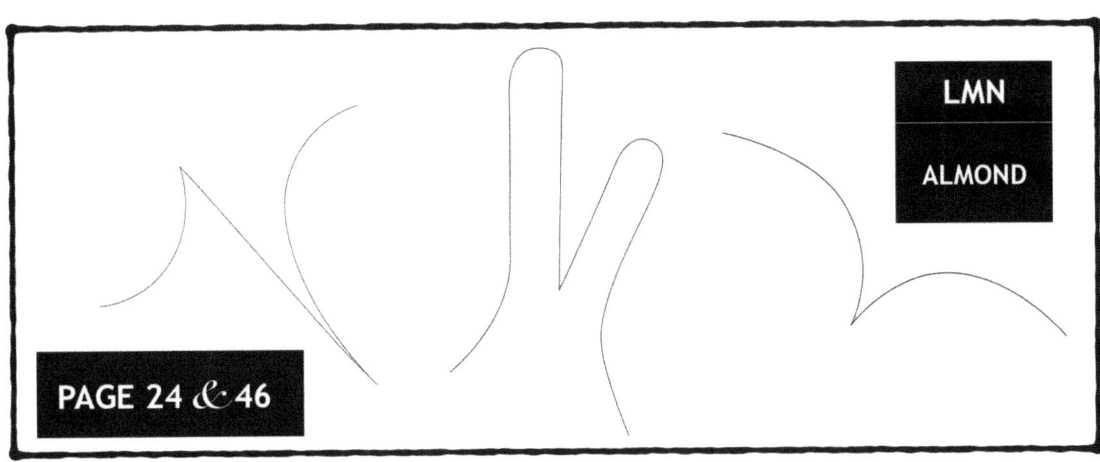

LMN
ALMOND

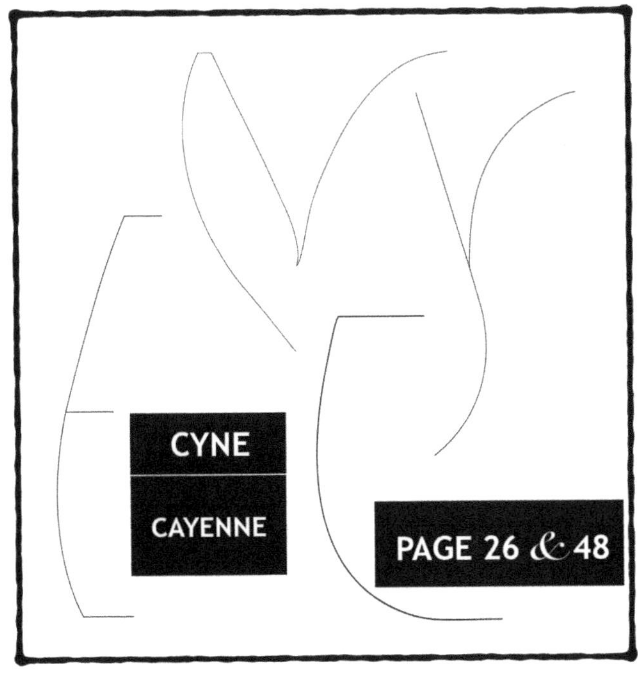

CYNE
CAYENNE

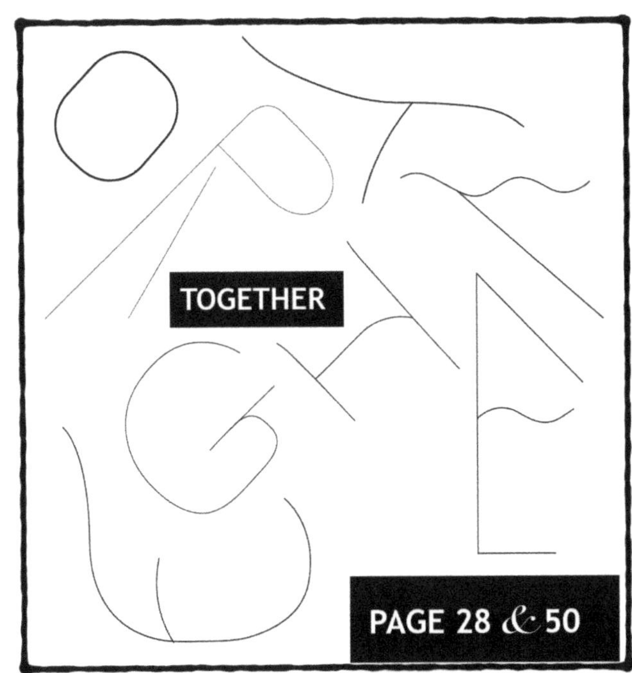

TOGETHER

Letters in Concert   Letters in Concert   Letters in Concert   Letters in Concert   Letters in Concert

Letters in Concert   Letters in Concert   Letters in Concert   Letters in Concert   Letters in Concert